et

veritas

ORDINARY, MOVING

Phyllis Gotlieb

Toronto
OXFORD UNIVERSITY PRESS
1969

For
LEO, MARGARET, JANE
and the rest of the world's children

PUBLICATION OF THIS BOOK WAS ASSISTED BY THE CANADA COUNCIL

Printed in England by
HAZELL WATSON AND VINEY LTD
AYLESBURY, BUCKS

CONTENTS

ORDINARY, MOVING

Before I was born, when
heaven was far but somewhere
they sang in the village I
never knew
in Krasilevka, in Anatevka
in the magic town of Chelm
suburb to the gravestone cities
of the pogrom dead:

Tell me, Rabbi, what will happen
when the Messiah comes?

:We will make a Festival
when the Messiah comes

What will be given us to eat
at that Festival?

:Wild-buffalo and Leviathan-meat
at that Festival

1

THE MORNING PRAYERS OF THE HASID, RABBI LEVI YITZHOK

Levi Yitzhok :
binding tefillin on
arm head hand till his spirit shone :
and his forehead burned
black and white in the light
of the eastern sun :
sang
   Good morning : good morning
   dear God : little Father :
   I beg You : hear the prayer of :
   Levi Yitzhok : son of Sara
   hear the prayer of
   Levi Yitzhok
   son of Sara
   Rabbi of Berditchev, disciple of
   : Dov Baer
always blinded by the light of God Levi
Yitzhok eyes opened wide
to the countryside of Heaven
                       Lord!
Your petitioner :
will not move from here :
from this place

son of Sara : Rabbi of
Berditchev will not move or stir
till You come to account with us!

for Your promises
are bound on the brows of Your children
and Your children
are the phylacteries of Your brow;

there are angels : made of fire and snow
who may sing Your praises more
than the one who prays before You
: Levi Yitzhok :

but do angels ask forgiveness?
and are angels beaten to dust?
are they killed by men and eaten
by pigs in the streets of Berditchev?

when my son died : I sent You in return
a spirit pure
as the one You lent me
a handful of years
: do angels cry till the tears
run through their fingers?
    I live only to magnify
    Your name and fill the world with
    Your presence
as Your worshipper :
Your petitioner :
Levi Yitzhok :
son of Sara
as a
Jew
who took Your Torah
when You hawked it in the marketplaces of the world!

till Your feet were sore and dusty
and the gold wore off the cover
and the parchments turned musty—

remember! only Moses
clasped it like a lover!

people of czar and emperor
people of king and throne
turned away the Law
we made our own!

shema Yisroel adonoy
elohenu adonoy echod
we have no king
we have no King but God!

for we wandered with Your promises
in the lightning of Your Law
by the hand from the pillar of fire
the voice from the burning
bush, the face in the cloud
   as mountains are bowed
   before the Lord
   so is Your servant
: Levi Yitzhok
: and a son of Yours
: Levi Yitzhok
             for is not my son Ephraim
my delight though I speak against him?
I will have mercy upon him, surely
and I will remember him

adonoy echod
there is no King but God

beardneedled grey & black silk caftan
: Levi Yitzhok danced and sang
angels watching from Paradise laughed and
climbed down rungs of light and the laughter
filled the rooms to rooftree pushed out
teacher disciple pupil

deafened argument agreement pilpul
dishes clapped hands walls clashed cymbals
samovar turned to beaten
gold and the fire rose and bowed
silver in every ember
: and a thousand miles below
: below in his red sty Satan

clasped black wings over ears closed eyes and
shivered in every member :

adonoy echod
there is no King but God

Who will bless us with his wisdom
at that Festival?

: Solomon the King will give the blessing
Moses the Rabbi will teach us Torah
David the King will play the psalter
Miriam the Prophetess will dance before us
at that Festival

A COMMENTARY

Good morning, the old man says
good morning toward the
yeshiva in heavystep
bookbag clasping
books in black letters blacker
than the ovens of Auschwitz lettershapes
crimped round thought/tongues of fire
his eyes are
wetstones
his beard splayed, in shoe heavystep
he smokes, breathes, breathsmoke
pillars the air
good morning:
melamed,

on Saturday morning
melamed, good Shabbas, he
brings home a minyan
of Hasidim for l'chaim

l'chaim!

in black :
caftans, fur shtreimlach : white
stockings : swung sidecurls :
pink flesh : black
asphalt green leaves : yellow sunlight blue
sky they come
step : walk
in a black flock pass

from pane to pane black
brown pink white black brown pink
white betweengreen
aisles of glass

when I go by the school where
minds may be narrowed I see
the yard a hundred Jewish children
laugh yell and raise hell
red blue green yellow

eyes like washed stones
splayed beard, a bringer of Hasidim
spreads the leaves of his prayers for them
: *this is an aleph*
his children have succumbed to Cyclon B

the old man smiles
good morning

good morning!
　　　　　　　from Lubavichi, Lublin
Bratzlav, Berditchev : Berlin
from Modzitz, Mezrich, Bialystock
Fastov, Opatov, Lodmir, Lodz

: ghostmarch in the noon of night
from pane to pane black brown pink white
betweengreen
aisles of glass

and over the Sabbath bread they sang:

The Rabbi Elimelech
called out his cymbal-player
: Our joy will serve the Lord
for every song is heard
and every sound is prayer

*

the day that I was born
no star shook itself
no comet vectored the heavens
the earth turned once on its axis
smoothly; embryo, foetus, birth
after some hesitation begins to breathe

THE CHILD THE TCHELITCHEW THE TREE

hide & seek
says Tchelitchew, the world's
a dandelion's eye
the hand child branches the
embryo root, red
shining head and

one, two, three
says Tchelitchew, the
child's the tree

balanced between fear and
joy, the shapes
of children turn the tree
from sun to earth and back
a lattice dark/day/light

I spy
with my eye
how the night
pulls down the sky

I stayed three nights
beside her bed
don't let the moon
touch me, she said

and Tchelitchew said, I eschew
the cold blue
pigment of the moon

(because he knew
the tree of bone)

there is no terror here, says
Tchelitchew, you do not know
that does not lace your vision's vein
your vascular
privateflowered tree

and he chose red and yellow
skybluepink & green

one, two, three
Peggy Lee
, sing a rainbow in a tree

the hand hides, but the child
pushes through dandelion-
eyed, preposterously red
blueveined embryonic head
to bring the light, to salt the tree
to be the word against the dead

9

some stop in darkness and are
remnants, unpersoned

IN THE LABLIGHT

the embryos in jars
have sad imprisoned faces
though they are beyond wars
naughtmen inside walls
they have no navels, only
roughcut umbilicals

dream not under the kind
amnion but the moon
of the eye's microtome
knives will extrude their causes
neither tide nor wind
move them, not even
nightmare; they have no marvels

: Play, children, play
the time for song is short
and age and sorrow come like frost
to wither up the heart

★

Fibonacci found the significance of
1, 1, 2, 3, 5, 8, 13 . . . ,
they explain
the way seeds spiral in the sun
flower and pine scales
twist in the cone

I tell you LYNDHURST 8325
means the house my aunt moved from in 1942
and I remember the cousins who said 20 years ago:
call us when you're in town, the number's
ILLINOIS 8-3713
but I forget their names

SO LONG IT'S BEEN

time to clear the silent
sullen round of numbers stacked in my
brainracks
        clear HOWARD 0141 where the one
armed man lived next door and Mrs Goldfarb
with her slipstraps slid on her fat pink arms
                        clear
HARGRAVE 8375 where the park sweeps below the railing
and Broadview Ave, on a foggy day a ship's
deck sailing a sea of limbo washed with
3 old skaters 7 tennis players and a shattered
rubbydub
        GERRARD 6715 Good evening Century Theatre

Goodbye Mrs Gersten, Miss Fernandez, Miss Fleuhrer &
all burglars anonymous uncaught who tied up my
father & stole the safe, or his lunch, or sometimes
even $$$$

           clear GERRARD 2222 (too) easy to remember *Call
me anytime* Mr Wallace walks me in the schoolyard &
knowing does not tell me my grandmother

                           LAKESIDE 0007
never liked flowers because they reminded her of
funerals: how many roses from hers have I found
cracking the backs of Uncle Nissel's
SCHUYLER 4-7767 old encyclopedias?

                        clear GROVER 9595
where I pulled the kid cousin's braids, ate
knishes, and cried: yes, he's dead, he died this
morning

           numbers that lived in me clear clear clear no
answer, nobody lives
there any more

my ghost directories are
yellowpage clear through, the
crossroads of the past
are one-way thoroughfares

★

the district where I live was raw
as a turned stone when I moved in
                              the houses
were planted and left to weather
and the children outstripped the trees; because
you already know the old man from Auschwitz
extrapolate Mrs Rosenzweig
who soaps her sidewalk
and her night's counterpart

CRAZY CLEAN LULLABY

the midnight brush goes cush cush cush
on the street where I live longalive flash flash
ing orange twirlight the midnight monster
scrubs the curb suburb nice nice howls
up the one and down the twice
growls sing a song along a lullaby baby lies
brushacry baby & turn not a hair
for sweeting the street
so sweep so fair

the street has no colour of its own
but for its leaves bricks and sky
birth and death stand at either end
and love and sorrow move between

lacking an OUR TOWN *or even an* OUT OUR WAY
you have to kneel down
with your eyes to the grass and draw
aesopian conclusions
from ink and arthropoda

A PICNIC OF PEDANTS

etymology's words
                    entomology
bugs. near as no difference, ant
looks a word, quarters
leaves, carries
weight.
            centipede a very
myriapod
            maybe dip a
spider in ink and produce
calligraphy, if you prefer
or
pick a word: for instance
etymology unlimber-
ing curly legs
and and and and and and and
scrawling across this page

once, only once, the King of the Cats
led his troupe in a pack, like rats
down the centre of this street
without music or magic, only once

PRESCIENCE

I know Cato will never pull
the weeds in my back garden
or Bunyan read Haggadah at my seder, I
will never pick olives from the groves of
Thales, or play
bezique with Lady Mary Wortley Montagu
nor will she split a hotdog at my barbecue; *we
shall receive no letters in the grave*
and I shall write you none, Sir!

                     but
perhaps a hundred years from now some
questive quoting X with an unfinished
thesis and an index yet to be collated will
miss my presence at a
live ungrieving ritual;

where's the fig will leaf this ground?
what brand of mandrake jump and shriek?

hardly one
         the November birds
feed on the fermented
berries of the mountain ash
and drunk do their best to brain themselves
on the pane's reflected sky
fall and lie trembling in the hedges
where children groan at their pulsing breasts
then feebly put on their ravelled wings
and stagger home to mend their heads

SUB ROSA

I don't know why, but robins choose
our crazy trellis-fence for the house
beautiful; stick straw string mud anything
goes, motherbird
deeps it with her bronze
burnisher; the secret hours out
4 copper sulphate globes kids
palm in sweaty hatchery while she
heads for the wormfront; one falls,
one vanishes, 2 wet nurslings break
shell, kids bear away empty
prizes, catspaw the begonias, fledglings
barbaric yawp earth & sky, kids
lift them, leave enriched
breadcrumbs in the murphy bed, motherbird
climbs the sunbeam, careless
as a mechanical
nightingale but
somehow
one
puffed
broody speckled
as an egg and ovoid youngster
survives kids going kitchycoo
and his cold bed, sums up the lot
                              become
thrice bigger than his dam, hangs around the
kitchen in his striped sweater, gulping
a slug now & then, a lubberly
caliban; well, she's
no momist, heaves the lout
over the side, he shrieks! scrunches in nakedeye

beam of the sun snivelling
for a soft featherwing of his ma, hops
here & there, weeps, noplacetogo, we chase
the fluffy lummox all round our yard
and the neighbours' scared of dogs, find
him a fencepost
                        trembles
grieves you'll-be-sorry, makes excuses, wets
his foot in the air and gets off
the pad at last;
                        merrywidow having flown the
coop lies open to the wandering
cuckoo

———

STAMP

unset cement's where the birdwalks
presses a leafshaped step
not quite the dinosaur he pigeon
toes hard by the Works Dep.

and goes, leaving a little
birdlime to mark the place
waiting for me to come, interpret
like a tracer of wildebeeste or
a talmudist in time

what it all meant that day (he swore,
was late home, feet sticky with the damn
stuff Product of Fazzola Bros., Contractors,
wife yapping he tracked her
clean floors, you
know the routine)

                        knock it off, bird,
        quit moaning, you got it all down
        hayfoot strawfoot, didn't you? you've
        gained an immortality
        in stone (almost) and
        also a critic (me)

        the seasons are reviewed
        as harshly by citizens and birds
        as if they might fail and fold
        leave their backers out of pocket
        and their world in its bare bones:

_____

BALLADE OF SPRINGSONG

Forsythia's pushed a sprig in the lee of the MOTOR
                        VEHICLES
LICENCES BRANCH, at the Marketeria they've put ripe
                        foreign
Jaffas out in tubs, the garden's got its full
growth on the backs of the seed envelopes
of radiant wax beans and pallid-bellied turnips, the sky
looks as if it could use a hosing-down, coming
down snow sometimes, like a rotten dirty trick, no
getting away from it, Spring's been going slumming

grass like the hide of an old mutt with the mange
hedge flowering with wipes of wet paper towel and pulped
kleenex in the wake of the garbage trucks gambolling down
the street yellow as dandelions, oh it'd give you the megrims
to hear the eclogues sung by starlings and crows
yammering with wind screaming
through screendoor, razzing round busted weatherstrip, no
question about it, Spring's been going slumming

I know trees never got a good foot in the earth from
dogs lifting a leg, waving broken branches
trying to pump threads of sap into their shreds of lives
sidewalks you can't step on for cracks and
pots in the road you could boil a terrapin
waiting for tar drip and steam humming
smooth, but you can't soothe frazzled insulted human
passions in a city where Spring's been going slumming

Lord, I'm glad to have eyes to see and ears to hear
the goods of earth and air, it's a shame a young
kid like Spring has to hold her nose and wear
black glasses in the city like a dowager gone slumming

there are commodities
apples oranges and artichokes
from all corners of the world
always in season
and from all corners of the spirit
there are commodities

IN SEASON

I watch
        chameleons and
children, children and
chameleons: one
elegant appetite sheds
skin every three weeks or
so, slits
seam on his tooth edge
spine bump grind and
shimmies around till he
stands loosened in the trans
lucent shimmy of his own skin
shoots cuff sloughs grabbing
with claw, gobbles it
down to save protein and swift
flick-switches to try out
the same brown/green he started
with
      children
writhing yearning and striving
hoicked up by jerky inches
measured wristbare and pantsleg
put out rawbone joint sweat gland
sex stirring trying to sow miracles
without seed casing the raw still
power, bust
clothes knee elbow & prat &
jettison ragged shirt, wracked
shoe leavings of outcast
armories
         how pectoral grooves the steel
breastplate shapes of the warm

skin form them
               in season I watch
them outgrow my arms

and if the seasons fall and fail
who shall put them right?

this is for the mother and the father
for the son they loved and his
songs flowers and streams

FOR JOHN ANDREW REANEY

Tell me your one-o
green grow the rashes-o
I'll tell you one-o
One is one and God's alone and ever more shall be so

Tell me your two-o
I'll tell you truly-o
fire-winged butterfly, eye-tailed peacock
shimmer in the field where the wildflowers grow
tell me your one-o
I'll tell you one-o
One is one and God's alone and ever more shall be so

Tell me your three-o
I'll tell you lovingly
three, three the starwhite petals of the lily
blowing in the wind on a stalk of living green-o
One is one with God alone and ever more shall be so

Four, tell me four-o
green grow the rashes-o
springleaf, Juneflower, treefall, snow
colour the meadow green blue and yellow
toadflax, chicory, Queen Anne's Lace, O
One, One, God alone and ever more shall be so

Sing me your five-o
: five alive-o
five are the gates that open to the spirit
ear to hear music, mouth to tell love
the hand that caresses, the eye that blesses
the sense of the soul as it ever more shall be so

Six, tell me six
green grow the rashes-o
six are the walkers winding to eternity
bearing their blessings as lightly as love
five are the senses-o
four are the seasons-o
One is one and God's alone and ever more shall be so

Tell me your seven-o
I'll give you seven
seven are the Shepherds who stand before the Lord
Adam, Seth, Methuselah, Abraham, Jacob, Moses
and David with his psalter who sang before the Ark: O
God is One and One alone and ever more shall be so

Eight, now, eight
eight the April rainers
swelling the streams that sing along the stones-o
seven are the Shepherds
six are the walkers
One is one and God's alone and ever more shall be so

Nine, tell me nine-o
green grow the rashes-o
nine are the Angels aureoled in Heaven
white as the daisies in the fields of morning-o
eight are the April rains the Shepherds are seven

Give me your ten-o
I'll give you One
ten are the Commandments blazed on living stone
I'll tell you One that's love and love alone
for God is love and love alone and ever more shall be so

Green grow the rashes-o
I'll tell you of eleven
who climbed the steps to Heaven
with their heads crowned in light
and their weary sandals worn
scarred in their martyrdom
turned to Jerusalem
One is God and God is love and ever more shall be so

Twelve, twelve, tell me your twelve
twelve are the flame-haired Apostles of the ceilings
burning in blue with peacocks at their feet, O
now tell your twelve-all

green grow the rashes-o
here are my twelve-all

goldrobed Apostles who tread their fields of blue
all, all but one have climbed the steps of Heaven
ten are the Commandments carved on stone
nine are the angels that God made in the morning
eight April rainers turn the fields to clover
seven are the Shepherds who bring the lambs to cover
six are proud walkers who guard their gift of blessing
five are the senses that open to the spirit
four are the seasons that turn upon their cycles

three, three the lilies that stand on stems so green-o
where peacocks shimmer and butterflies hover
run, child, run where the fields are rich with clover

One is one and God's alone and ever more shall be so!

it is the merry month of May
the springtime of the year
and we have come into your house
to taste of your strong beer

and if you have got no strong beer
we'll be content with small
we'll take the goodwill of your house
and give God thanks for all

a branch of May we bring you
that at your door doth stand
it's but a sprout well budded out
the work of our Lord's hand

*our song is done, we **must be** gone*
no longer can we stay
*God bless you all, both **great** and small*
we wish you happy May

★

it was midnight on the ocean
not a streetcar was in sight
I walked into a drugstore
to try to get a light
the man behind the counter
was a woman old and grey
who used to peddle shoestrings
on the road to Mandalay

ON THE BUS FROM TRUE TO FALSE

up front light was rose all the way
because the sides were green and
eye turned green white
green snow's not true, not right
through spattered
fibrecolour snow got smutted &
sun stainface

        sun
glass cheaters of colours I eschew I
ask of the pane: will you at least show
me a wild Oz? if not true snow? but
no, it's all bile & jaundice

            turn
away to melancholy
seatbacks, an aislebound child's

whimpering; in front the windshield's blind
pink, the compensatory
eye complements distortion, finally distorts
the real, so nothing's true here,
nothing
          the child
out of the blue asks me if I like
Green Eggs & Ham oh yes, oh yes
(but why?)
not green snow, green sky

it's a bird, it's a plane, it's a
pain in the neck, it's a thorn
in the flesh, it's

A CATFUL OF BUTTERMILK

nothing, a family saying, like for
enough is enough, enough already! *yoysher!*
a bellyful, something turning queasy, storm
brewing, gorge rising, that's when
you say enough is a
catful of buttermilk

when you've got a spirit
ache like an ague
of the bones, when the sky
pushes down like the
lid of a garbage-can and all

words ring down a fall of
lead nickels, the old
gnaw their gums and blink and the
wind is a wolves' bite in the thigh

the hue and cry out at the graves
of the unnumbered
dead riding in their careers
in turn howling a hollow
tolling from hell
                    can we
crawl down to the cat from here
and the buttermilk?

Prince, President, Prime
minister, Premier, Potentate,
Pontifex, Pasha, Panjandrum & Pooh-bah, ah
the hell with it, it's a
catful of buttermilk

almost a ballade because
mixed with the Baudelaire & bagels
it has a soupçon of Villon
the hardknock blackguard with the skull's grin
my virtuous youth loved: soulblack & redhot with sin
3 vols., half-leather, marbled endpapers
his shifting marble eyes turnspits of fire, a
leatherboy in weathered skin pinching
his fat maggot Margot and
never coming in
out of the rain

1. PROVERBS

Enough butting, you bust your head
enough dipping, the pitcher breaks
enough firing, the iron turns red
enough hammering, you get cracks
enough running and you make tracks
enough goodness, you'll pull out plums
enough naughtiness, you get smacks
enough calling and Christmas comes

enough talking and you'll raise doubt
enough fame and you'll find the claques
enough promises, you'll back out
enough wishing, maybe it takes
enough boozing, you get the shakes
enough starving, you gobble crumbs
enough gobbling, your belly aches
enough calling and Christmas comes

enough howling, you feed the mutt
enough buzzing and you'll make wax
enough keeping, the apples rot
enough picking and you'll break locks
enough dithering, your luck croaks
enough hurry and you're all thumbs
enough betting, you lose the stakes
enough calling and Christmas comes

enough nagging, you should drop dead
enough spending, you're on the rocks
enough kindness, you're out of bread
enough promises won't mend socks
enough faith will move bricks and blocks
enough lending, you'll beg for dimes
enough blowing will blow down oaks
enough calling and Christmas comes

Prince: enough humbling, a fool chokes
enough living, what's left of dreams?
enough rope—there's no time for jokes!
enough calling and Christmas comes

no joke: in 1461
yearning on friends he hadn't got
groaning with syph, racked with TB
he shrank between sweating walls
under the moat at Meung-sur-Loire
on some scraped-up charge; good riddance
to a thief and pimp
who's far too handy with a knife

to bring him in focus for myself
I moved him down 500 years and
east 5000 miles

2. EIN BREVE TSU ZEIN CHAVERIM

Won't anybody have pity on me?
can't you hear me out there any of you?
friends I'm depending on? jump in the sea!
Stuck in a ditch! What did I ever do
to deserve you—yes you, tearing a shoe
with the Hasidim; try it here, instead
and you'll find out! Long as your belly's fed
and you pick up a penny here and there
maybe you think I'm on a featherbed?
I ask you, can you leave me lying here?

It's so dark you could go blind; who can see
through stone walls? the quiet's like deafness; blue
sky and wind mean nothing to you: you're free—
I'm a bone in the bottom of a stew
pot, a fly buzzing in a pot of glue;
you're home guzzling borsht till your beards are red
—and my beard's red with blood! you're stuffing bread
and bagels; sure, you'll boil me chickens, sure,
you'll make me soup with farfel—when I'm dead!
I ask you, can you leave me lying here?

Come on, if you have any decency,
look what I'm in, here, and if you're not too
busy gnawing the toothpick, bring a key.
I get a crust that every time I chew
it, I lose a tooth, when they want to know
something they don't ask me nicely, they flood
my gut with water . . . I'm already glad
Tuesdays when they make me a Yom Kippur
and also Fridays . . . hungry, cold, afraid
I ask you, can you leave me lying here?

Tsarevitch, if you do the will of God
please let me go! The others let me bleed.
They're worse than pigs. Pigs, at least, if they hear
one squeal, they all come running . . . do I need
to beg you? Will you leave me lying here?

maybe my grandfathers knew
a goniff or two like him in the
Czar's army

he scraped through that and
one or two more squeaks and
vanished in a void
and nobody knew where he'd gone
or if he plied the bitter trade
but God & F. Villon

3. SMALL TALK

I know how milk gets full of flies
I know apples fall near the tree
I know the weather by the skies
I know men by their vanity
I know the honey from the bee
I know the worker from the drone
I know you can't get off scot free
I know all spirits but my own

31

I know some lovers by their sighs
I know some jackets by their fleas
I know some thieves with shifty eyes
I know monks by their rosaries
I know nuns by their modesties
I know good wine by cask and tun
I know when fools are full of cheese
I know all spirits but my own

I know how pigs live in their sties
I know how fish come from the sea
I know two bits and what it buys
I know Matilda and Marie
I know of sleep and fantasy
I know the Pope, I know the Throne
I know of faith and heresy
I know all spirits but my own

Prince, I know all diversity
I know the flesh, I know the bone
I know how death will feed on me
I know all spirits but my own

perhaps he was hanged; he'd
escaped by a hair so often
some believe he went to England
                              perhaps
he's alive and living on the Riviera

but I think he died in a ditch
with the grey sky pressing on the snow
wolves barking over the fields, his
knees drawn up bared through the torn hose
teeth bared through flesh, their chattering
stopped with ice, his bones at last
bared, turning
toward the earth where they began

I ASK YOU

Suppose Catullus had lived on and on
an aging boy, never quite growing up?
always sure of a jug to fill the cup
a hand to pour it and a redeye dawn?
supposing Keats had married Fanny Brawne
shrugged off TB and in a chemist's shop
while the harsh tinctures gathered drop by drop
dreamed a new wild way-out Endymion?

and if Byron had come back from his war
and written I WAS THERE and SEE IT NOW
would ancient toothless Burns, pushed to the edge
by fifty women, long for the lost plough?
would roaring Brendan meekly sign the pledge?
and Dylan, sobered down, take up guitar?

in Stratford Churchyard W★ll Sh★k★sp★★r★
I think with the odd English slantblue eyes
(or pointbeard Oxford if you like, Bacon
in starched ruff or the great Queen herself in
jewelled stomacher & taffeta farthingale)
hunkered by grave-edge watches sexton dig

: How long will a man lie i'th'earth 'fore he rot?

: Faith, if 'e be not rotten wi' pox 'fore 'e die sh'd
last you some eight year; a tanner will last you nine.

: Why he more than another?

: Faith, 'is hide's so tanned with 'is trade 'e'll
keep out water a great while—haw!

                               drunk on his own wit
gapmouth his face catches fire from his red nose and
flames out to its circumference
like Bardolph's
                 but W★ll
touches sceptre-thigh & picks up orb skull:

                         O
this had a tongue in't and could sing once . . .

A DISCOURSE

the skeleton's the most articu-
late thing there is except
about Who made him. It's not
graveyards he rattles in but
you and me; skeletons
chase butterflies and do the
Monster Mash in the dark infra-
redroom of the flesh

               starting
from the grounded arches of
Man's first pedestal the
Tarsals and Phalanges bones
baby needs shoes for, not
the ones that get them,
keystones for

            legs of
concern to dashers and prancers
stylers and milers fencers fandancers
romancers advancers
and retreaters
               unsinewed a collection
of bones named after
skillets and safety pins

              the Femur
the skeleton's oaktree, in the old
soon broken least mended
has little to recommend it
in a poem except in the thunderclaptrap
of one lowly notch called the Intercondylar
and one lordly knob called the Greater Trochanter

while Pelvis itself ugly needs flesh
to notify it yet a crown of bones
in the woman the royal
colander drains
life from the sea
waters of the uterine cavern

and
the tailbone, Coccyx well
named after the cuckoo
connects with old jokes of banana
peels but the Pelvis
attaches that column of latin
the spine, at the Sacrum

in form
eschew connotations of
ramrod or spinelessness, choose
for symbol the integral
S-shaped, both practical and pleasing; here are
integers stacked like
lecture chairs but cushioned in use
always; muscles may atrophy but these
let heads held high
glare each other in the eye
and swear

rising out of lumbago country and its young
ambassador absorbine junior
through thorax the Dorsals
seem to belong to dolphins
rather than the ribcage
called cavity crammed with vitals

the seven bars of the neck
noted for the top two that help
you nod or shake
so superbly lubricated only
the heart goes creak

the Hyoid hangs out
in this district, a bone
without visible means of support
silent and anonymous in
the mugbook of the anatomist

but the arms have apparatus!
clefshaped Clavicle
doubles the spine's integral
over the stave of the Ribs most
graceful of all body
spans from Sternum to Scapula a
flat plate and the base of wings in angels
armsocket in Mankind;

the humerus: enough said;

Radius and Ulna are staff and support
for that fan that pinwheel that unbeached
starfish the hand: I think of arms raised
lotus columns of Egypt
buttressed by shouldermuscle
and finally fingers touching tips
over the Skull, full
circle from the Phalanges we began with

the Skull's the pontine
arch of the pontifex homely
to me, the only one I met

in person, as a child
                    my medschool
cousin used a sawed-off
skulltop for ashtray I thought
the flakes inside were dried remains
of brains, bonepink shocked me reading
so much of desert alkali but knew
the concave brainshape volutes cup
cortex and arteriole

                    when
you put your lefthand
fingers into the inter
stices of your right is how
the Frontal fits the Parietals
in the noble Cranium the base
doesn't look that neat
but none the less suffices

                    the
Ethmoid takes the weight
of the great oracle with its flutes and coils
Temporals remind us
how bound to time we are Zygomatics
give children those apple
cheeks
        leave Sphenoid
Conchae, Palatines all fragile none
termed ephemeral for

Stapes, Malleus, Incus
the Auditory Ossicles a
tone poem of their own tell you
what goes bump in the night, usually
the kid falling out of bed on his
Occiput

from here the Foramen Magnum opens the door
from the brain to the neural telegraph
lines strung along the vascular
tree in lands I have no visa for

balled in a burlap of triple
membranes the rooty
brain's a thing contained and only
container of everything best left
cased under the lock and key of its senses

bridge span arch imply
traffic
        in the complex I
admire most the Foramina piercing
bone where marrow hatching phagocytes knock on the wall
arcades where nerve and vein pass through
providentially
and begin to define the flesh

the spirit's limits have their arbiters
but I know where the devil
starts

a blink inside the skull?
the brain creaks too

DEATH'S HEAD

at 3 a.m. I run my tongue
around my teeth (take in a breath)
(give out a breath) take one more step
approaching death. my teeth are firm
and hard and white (take in a breath)
incisors bite and molars grind
(give out a breath) the body lying
next to mine is sweet and warm
I've heard that worms (take in a breath)
don't really eat (give out a breath)
the coffin meat of human kind
and if they did I wouldn't mind
that's what I heard (take in a breath)
(and just in time) I think it's all
a pack of lies. I know my flesh
will end in slime. the streets are mean
and full of thieves. the children in
the sleeping rooms (give out a breath)
walk narrowly upon my heart
the animal beneath the cloth
submerged rises to any bait
of lust or fury, love or hate
(take in a breath) my orbic skull
is eminently frangible
so delicate a shell to keep
my brains from spillage. still my breath
goes in and out and nearer death

and yet I seem to get to sleep

NOTHING

tonight I have an empty mind
there is nothing naught aught in it anything
my eyes are as vacant as bubbles
my ears are scrolls borrowed from gingerbread cornices
tongue a tissue of the impalpable improper
I write only to keep my pen from clogging and my
arm from atrophying

I have nothing to fill nothing with but blood bones breath
pulses and traces for the encephalograph
a heart cut from red lace paper flutters
absurd as a bird in the bag of the pericardium

a head of hair full of air an
eggshell skull a pleated brain
prepackaged in cellophane mucosity a dura mater
thin as a linen handkerchief and insubstantial
atomdance in a void of velocity

oh it's a nudnik nothing night a sniveller a snuffer
of joie de vivre you could turn my
dissenting decentralized reticular structure to a
rebus a ratchet a rocket a tower of babel a ring
around a rosy upsydaisy arsyversy

(what did I tell you?)
nothing

★

I had this piano-piece called Albumblatt
it was so melancholy-sweet it'd
make the tongue stick to the roof of your mouth

I turn leaves and the pictures crackle
lined in brownfaded uniform configuration
Bloom forehead and Rosenblatt nose so
repetitive bone for bone and cartilege for cartilege
you'd swear the wet flesh was pressed in the hard mold
all dead but one: a kitchentable kid
remembers Aunt Sarah in her perfume cloud
wit grace & bawdymouth delight
blowing in from her roaring city

A BALLAD OF 2 VOICES, N.Y.

Aunt Sarah:
I started life on 3rd St.
where whores and perverts flourished
I ran from them on the legs
soup & farfel nourished

Phyllis:
Why is the bearded
man alone with his coat folded neat-
ly on the greengrass bouncing
a ball on the parkpath?

Aunt Sarah:
my mother wore a sheitel
my father wore a tallith
they blinked blind eyes at voyeurs
what did they know of brothels?

Phyllis:
the young browndown counter
man sprouts from his allhands
plate knife fork *zip!*
cups like capuchins leap
from his frondpalms

Aunt Sarah:
my father dug in the subway pit
an immigrant with a barrow
my mother baked pletzlach
and lifted the fallen sparrow

Phyllis:
O am I blessed
(plink)? is a tear
drop from an angel of God
falling on my forehead or
only a drip from an
overhead airconditioner?

Aunt Sarah:
I had a husband, fed
a son who fought in a place
I never heard of; he died
with madness in his face

Phyllis:
young Negro girls go down-
town at a strut, jut-
ting out breast & backside, en-
joying what they've got

Aunt Sarah:
my husband, my son are dead
my parents far buried
I hate the city I loved in
it's an apache I married

Phyllis:
it's the Friedsam
carousel, ringading where I
get my nostalgi@ 2 for 2 bits I'm
putting a clause in my will ringading, for the children of
Time, for the silver and gold
of my love ringading
for the children, the silver
the gold . . .

Aunt Sarah:
I was mugged in my own street
I lay like a cursed stone
but I'm tough as the city that grew me
I die by the inch alone.

she and her four dead brothers limbs
of my Tchelitchew-tree
the rough brash of their voices
a wind echo in a dream

★

just the other day I found
this old clipping in a drawer
creased yellowed faded as my albumblatten
recording an interview with a local
poetess & authoress (the name is accidentally
torn away) and the whole thing is rather
ragged because it was picked out with a
blunt toothpick:

    terviewed in her comfortable suburban h
ffording a fine view of the hou
      oss the street, over a cup o
    ightly stale coffee, lounging comfortably i
        fth Yoga position and dres
    ust a few things I happened to fling on," sh
aid with an uneasy l
      eally if you want to know about m
nd my writing and what I think about s
        itics and things like tha
      gest you take a look a
    at I've written ab
       oodness! the soup

FIRST PERSON DEMONSTRATIVE

I'd rather
heave half a brick than say
I love you, though I do
I'd rather
crawl in a hole than call you
darling, though you are

I'd rather
wrench off an arm than hug you though
it's what I long to do
I'd rather
gather a posy of poison ivy than
ask if you love me

so if my
hair doesn't stand on end it's because
I never tease it
and if my
heart isn't in my mouth it's because
it knows its place
and if I
don't take a bite of your ear it's because
gristle gripes my guts
and if you
miss the message better get new
glasses and read it twice

IDENTITIES FOR SHADOWCHASERS

Ego; me; I; my
                    shadow's
very well anchored, thank
you, my tears are in
glass boxes, when I cry I
know it's my miauling not
the cat's, when I'm
scared 32 knackers clack like
castanets, when I love my
kiss laps the cheeks of the sun, when

my anger flies off the handle it's got
lieb engraved on the blade
                              don't think my
shadow's so feeble I don't have to
give it a wrestle, my tears are
nitric sulphuric or what
ever corrosive
thing you can think of, when I
let out a shriek would crack the
roof of your denture you can bet your
life you'll remember

                         and when the axe of
my dreams hacks at the rooftree of self I
grow round it helve deep in my pitted
breast where many a
hatchet's buried. So

if your shadow won't stick on your back don't bother
running to me I don't need a
patch on the dark already
tucked in my guts when I've got sky
hooks in my skull
to hold down the
day

SOLITAIRE 37½

I lay out the words like cards in caracols
trying to toss them a life that pricks and stings
do they stay in the air like the juggler's ringling balls?
my juggler's a joker moping in the wings
with a busted slapstick. I want riotings
and all the heyrube and racket of carnivals?
the deuces are tame and all the cocks doxies king
queens cullies knaves of the pack that flicks and falls

I swear I tear my hair I crawl the walls
every time I try to shuffle the things
flat on their backsides smiling painted dolls
—and you were so full of flesh and beckonings
blood beating bickering and fist thumpings
ten minutes ago! where's the fishwife bawls
you were yelling in my ears? cocks doxies kings
queens cullies knaves of the pack that flicks and falls

all paper and scratch lagging and lophead lolls
get on your hind legs! argue the reckonings!
maggoty miching, where's the moxie? molls
natter and knit bleatings and gibberings
dithering in the tangles of their strings
rocks in their heads bellyflop creeps and crawls
what have you done for me lately? cocks and kings
queens cullies knaves of the pack that flicks and falls

okay Prince, kick it up and the word sings
pinch till it hollers, live it up scrapes and scrawls
what have you got for an encore doxies kings
queens cullies knaves of the pack that flicks and falls?

GOING CRITICAL

For a start set their teeth on edge

fill their days with falling buttons & stuck zippers
holes in their socks and menders with nervous
fingers who knot them
raw hangnails & dull clippers

let them sweat in their twisted sheets with horrible
dreams of the knacker; give them post-nasal drip
make them allergic to oxygen nitrogen xenon; put their
Cough Control Centres entirely out of whack

give them cinders in their eyes gutgripes & palpitations
an itch in the Eustachian tubes where they can't scratch
and whichever their sex
give them pre-menstrual tension!

let them retch
when everything's spewed like a ten times seasick traveller
ringworm wherever it's possible to get it, give them
tapeworm & hookworm where you can get that
and anything else there's worms for, any
small sniggering snivelling miserable bit
and if there's space left over pox acne & impetigo
scab them around like the dry bites of lizards

give them a sense of being encircled by buzzards
on watch for their bones, in slow lazy drifts
in those bones
give them agues & fevers and if the poor buzzards
want rest let them
roost on their livers

and call down night darkness and hooded with flickering
clouds the spirits of mold mildew & migraine
bubble up in the pot and plague them a redhot
river of blast & scall rats bats lice and

oh yes

may their ears be tickled by musty
featherdusters forever

WHAT I SAW, WHAT I HEARD

I heard a man in the pit of hell
swear the fire was asphodel

I saw a man with a redhot harrow
gnawing his side; he said it was a sparrow

I knew a man with a cold steel stave
driven in his belly. He called it love.

while I am lying in bed counting my teeth
in the middle of the night or
casting dream-seines over the shore of the world
a mamenka in a babushka is eating
cucumbers and sourcream on the
Trans-Siberian to Vladivostok, a
bagelmaker with a long knife is whacking
white slabs from the dough-mountain to
chop, twist, boil, a sweetfaced
old lady in a strong leather glove
hauls down the knobfist arm of a

slotmachine in the GOLDEN NUGGET, &
rattles her plates for joy as the dimes
chime in the pot
                        and

                            somewhere
a fat bald bluejawed man in
carpetslippers pleats his hairy fingers
over his belly and snores gently, bluelit
by TV that whispers:

But General! Don't you understand?
this Martian xglummpk is the only alien life-form
we've ever had an opportunity to examine!
we must keep it alive!
we must! we must! WE MUST!

POP! GOES THE EASEL

What happened was
all the fathombeasts that ever bashed
the surface/tension of the
shadowscreen and the silent stealthy shadow
trackers of the killer and the brash ones too the
Bulldog/drummers and Maigret/regretters
Hammers of God/forsaken louts and loonies
King Kongs & Mings of Mongo
came up for air I mean
Pow! right off the page/screen/canvas
alive in simultaneous reality
on this the fairflower of our lambent
earth billboard & boxtop Wow! what

rowwracking nights we had
then, what adrenalin/docked days
running amok the concurrence of walleyed
thieves thugs yeggs mugs spivs till they'd
Docsavaged & Hairsbreadth/harried us, you & me
Bam! onto the page/screen/canvas Greatscott
& Ogeegosh we were

feelin no pain. I mean.
no pain.
no love. Nothing but
flicker & writhe in
2 constrained dimensions no
hailstones gallstones flintstones
were our weather our rage
decalcomania. That's how it crumbled.

Sometimes
they look/read/watch us strange
phenomena of their immaterial
age of ex
crescent dinosaurs & leaping
lizards. And turn away. We stir
no passions, Charley. If they grieve
guiltfingered
Bonds console them. So

kiss me quick before the fade
out and tell me
in one balloon, one frame
                              the way we
played it, what did we have Toulouse
Lautrec?

tonight
words are playing
in star haze under moon
seas over trove ships
                        there is a glitter
to them that is more facet-turning than water
joined they are molecules

moonglade an integer
I love and don't use
is the highway
of the moon on the sea
too elvish & spritely the trail
of the Blessed Damozel
                        no matter
it never spoiled
the element the dolphins reach in

DOLPHIN WALK

Take a scythe by the snath, swing
it, you cut a swathe
if it's sharp, take a
harp by the string, swing it, you
get heavenly
blues, take a wand in hand, wave it,
you get nothing much because
wishes don't come true

take a bird in the bush, flush
a pair of lovers, hush my
mouth, fill it with a silver
spoon, cry baby cry
it belongs to NASA, no use
reaching for the moon

take a stalk of wheat, stack it in a
stook, grab a ticker when nobody's
looking, swipe a clock, stick
a thumb on nose, wiggle fingers, you're
cocking a snook, and I'm
doing the dolphin walk.

I'm gonna lay my head on a lonesome railroad line
gonna lay my head right down on a lonesome railroad line
an let that two-nineteen train pacify my min'

PETRARCH'S SONNET

Saint Louis woman with her diamond rings
better peel her shadow offa my door
keep her hands off my man cause I get sore
hearin about her an her apron strings
says I aint got diamonds an all them things
only got what he always loved before
an all I got's what he don' want no more
give him to her an listen how she sings

leave me alone an go your ramblin ways
aint for me you chunkin that money roun
leave me so blue aint got the spit to die
never been so blue in all my born days
I'm tellin you baby dont ask me why
I hate to see that evenin sun go down

two-nineteen took my baby away
two-nineteen done took my baby away
two-seventeen bring him back some day

HAIKU AND $\frac{1}{2}$

erector, cherry-
picker, mother-
ship, umbilical
cord, the continuity
of the race
in space

born in a satellite orbiting Mars
one of the far-off evening stars
caught his braces on a passing rocket
that was the end of Davy Crockett

King of the Universe

*

here's how I spent my misspent youth
whether or not you want to know
like all writers listening
in buses cars & cafes
trams & subways
streets & alleyways:

says to her mabel i don't give a good god/got no feeling at all for him
anymore and he can do what he/should snow tonight i heard on/
mothers had a big fight and the wedding's/savin that plank for years an
went in the basement to look at it an it was all curled up like a rainbow
well i/you ╫ @ % ╫ $&ϕ !! you better gitcher/don't stop crying i'll
give you such a/thinks he can make me work after five o'clock he can
damn well

my brain the rainbarrel under the eavesdrop
every carstop a cram course
and I read: the walls of the world

DEBBIE LOVES (FRANKIE) (ELVIS) (RINGO) (MICK
JAGGER)/WE LOVE OUR LITTLE TOILET WE TRY TO
KEEP IT NEAT/MARIETTA REEKS WITH SMELL/BILLY
STINKS/SEX I LOVE YOU

and what have I got?
a brainful of rain and

come drink your wine in the shade of Mount Vesuvius
drop in and hoist a couple at Calpurnia's
come on, spend a sesterce, business is
booming in Pompeii!

OHNNY WATTERS CLUMB THIS WALL
NOBODY COME THIS HIGH AT ALL
I'LL STAY UP HERE UNTIL I FA

BOXCAR MOLLYS BEEN HERE
SHE GIVE THE BOYS SOME TIMES
BUT NOW SHES ROLLIN SOUTH
WHERE THE SUN ALLWAYS SHINES

Will's a scribbler, Ben's a sot
Kit's inclined to riot
Would they'd shift with pen & pot
And leave the MERMAID quiet!

I Neferkere King of Upper and Lower Egypt
await the coming of the Royal Explorer
Herkhuf who is bringing My Majesty a
pygmy from the Land of Punt
to play with I was
8 years old yesterday my
mother calls me
Pepy

YANKEE GO HOME!!!
KILROY WAS HERE!!!
BAN THE BOMB!!! RE
TRIBUTION IS NEAR!!!

I lived like a gent in the City
And I somehow neglected to pay
So goodbye Lucy dear, it's a pity
But I'm sailing for Botany Bay

IM HOLED UP 7 WK IN THIS SHACK
WITH RAIN & SNOW & BLIZZARD
AFORE THE RAILRD GITS ME BACK
I DRUTHER SLIT ME GIZZARD

You know the rhymester called Villon
A starveling crows would scorn to peck
But when he climbs the steps at dawn
His backside's weight will stretch his neck

I Huang Wei directed the
placing of stones in this
section. One more day on
mouldy rice and my
bones will also be part of
the Great Wall

s old Mother Hodge to be burnt for a witch
r the laying of curse & the casting of spell
ough I'm sure never harm came to any poor soul
om me & my coven! Greymalkin, farewell!

This room's reserved for LADIES
Though some that's been here aint
Or they would write with lipstick
& not scratch up the paint

AID 2 BITS FOR THIS HERE DOSS
WISH I HAD 3 SQUARES
Y BELLY THINKS MY THROATS CUT
UT THE BUGS IS GETTIN THERE'S

Rabbi, Inquisitor, mapmaker, bricklayer
what did you sing in the street?
what did you write on the wall?

kneescabber, hairpuller, gumsnapper, ropeskipper
nosepicker, pick up your feet
ballbouncer, lend me your ball:

one, two, three, four
Charlie Chaplin went to war

Charlie Chaplin went to France
to teach the ladies how to dance

lift your skirt and round you go
heel, toe, a-lairy-o!

ORDINARY, MOVING

is the name of the game
laughing, talking where the ball bounces
in the forgotten schoolyard
one hand, the other hand; one foot, the other foot
you know the one
(Saturday Afternoon Kid
blackball-cracker, scotchmint-muncher
handkerchief-chewer extraordinary)
clap front, clap back
ballthwack on the boardfence
front and back, back and front
arms of old beeches reaching over drop their
sawtooth leaves in your hair
   (as I was sitting beneath a tree
   a birdie sent his love to me
   and as I wiped it from my eye
   I thought: thank goodness cows can't fly)
tweedle, twydle
curtsey, salute
and roundabout
until you're out

the shadows turn, the light is long
and while you're out you sing this song

     this year, next year, sometime, never
     en roule-en ma boule roule-en
     we'll be friends for ever and ever

Pimperroquet, le roi des papillons
se faisant la barbe, il
se coupa le menton
une, une, c'est la lune
deux, deux, c'est le jeu
trois, trois—c'est à toi!

seven, eight
nine, a-laura
ten a-Laura
Secord

echod, shtaim
hamelech bashomayim
echod, shtaim, sholosh, ar-ba . . .

whereja get the cold, sir?
up at the North Pole, sir;
what were ya doin there, sir?
catchin Polar bears, sir;
how many didja catch, sir?
one, sir; two, sir

Salome was a dancer
she did the hootchykootch
she shook her shimmy shoulder
and showed a bit too much

my boyfriend's name is Fatty
he comes from Cincinnati

my boyfriend's name is Jello
he comes from Monticello

ini ini maini mo
que cheleque palestó
que jingale lestingó
ini ini maini mo

and this is the way you played
begin:

ordinary throw the ball against the fence, catch it
moving same thing, don't move your feet *laughing*
mustn't show your teeth *talking*
shut, your, mouth
                    one hand that's how you
catch it *the other hand*
one foot pick it up, you dope *the other foot*
and
clap front, clap back
                    front&back, back&front
tweedle with your hands like twiddling your thumbs
only overhand
twydle underhand *curtsey, salute*
and *roundabout*
                    catch it and
start from *moving*

over the whole thing without
stirring from the spot slap
your leg for *one foot* wave your
arms for *roundabout* on through *laughing* ononon

TILL YOU GET TO *BIG MOVING*!!!

particle, atom, molecule, world
solar system, galaxy, supergalaxy, cosmos

but start with small, the ball on the wall
that's how it went, and begin again:

  my boyfriend's name is Tonto
  he comes from New Toronto
  with twenty-four toes
  and a pickle on his nose
  and this is the way my story goes:

we
started
something
like   a   slug
and grew without
a thought or wish to
something like a fish a
frog a bird a pig a golly-
wog and ultimately red and
born a blueblack head or
peppercorn or bald or
blind or idiot or
multiheaded
,poly-
glot
★

$I = I$
$I? = ?I$
$?W?H?Y?$
$?I = I?$

$I = \text{not}$
ALL/eye/see
$= (s/m)\text{uch}$
$= \text{notme}$

(rockabye baby the cradle is hard
yer pa got it outa the junkman's backyard)

the thing that I thought was the moon
turned out to be Mother's face
or Sister's or Brother's or Dad's or the cat's
—there's notme all over the place

(but I want the world's food in my belly
I want all the things I can see
I want all the toys in the world in my arms
and I want all the arms around ME)

black skin, drum belly
little stick leg
Papa paint the sores on
hold your hands and beg

*

What shall we name the baby?
William? or James? or John?
Matthew? or Mark? or maybe
even Napoleon?

sticks and stones can break my bones
but names'll never hurt me
and when I'm dead and in my grave
you'll be sorry for what you called me

whatcher name?
Dickery Dame
ask me agin
and I'll tell ya the same . . .

. . . the secret power, the personal key
the three golden hairs in the forehead of the Giant
the stone in the yoke in the egg in the duck
in the rabbit in the basket in the chest beneath the Oak

in the Oak of the Golden Bough
in the magical Mistletoe:

'In the whole of the East Indian Archipelago
the etiquette is the same
no-one utters his own name . . .'

   sha-ame, sha-ame!
   everybody knows yer na–ame!

whatcher name?
Mary Jane
wheredya live?   comment t'appelle tu?
down'a lane   je m'appelle comme mon père
whatcher number?   et ton père?
cucumber   mon père s'appelle comme moi

it's Dinger Bell and Dusty Miller, Moishe Tochas
   and Lumber Bonce
it's *mwele* and Elkeh Pipick, Scaevola, Pepito and
   Tanglefoot . . .

what do they call 'y?
Patchy Dolly
where were y' born?
in the cow's horn

   *

where were ya born? I didn hear ya
roundabout and begin again
well I'll tell ya

   my father was born in England
   my mother was born in France
   but I was born in diapers
   because I had no pants

(cross my heart and hope to die
if I ever tell a lie)

where were you born my pretty lass?

born in the still-house bin
ifn Pappy hadn picked me outa the mash
they'd'a called me Stone Blind Gin

where do you come from, Cotton-Eye Joe?
way down south where the taters grow

where do you come from, Vinegar Bill?
where the Gila sleeps in the sagebrush hill

where do you come from, Popoli
in your *laplap* jockstrap sewn with bead?
I'm growing up in New Guin-ea
under the eye of Margaret Mead

laughing, talking, one hand, the other hand
one foot, the other foot
that's where the shoe is
roundabout

★

how's your old man earn his nicker?
potter? piper? peapod-picker?
packer? knacker? sailor? stoker?
bumbailiff? or bailbond-broker?
doctor? proctor? thane? or thief?
dustman? postman? on relief?

my old man's a dustman
he wears a dustman's hat—

aah, knock it off, Noddy
we already been there

my old man's a navvy
a navvy by his trade
he wheels a great big barrow
he swings a pick and spade

my old man's a navvy
he gets a navvy's pay
it doesn't fill a rotten tooth
or scare the wolf away

I'm growin up to earn my keep
as quickly as I can
an I guess I'll be a navvy
just like my old man

my father works in the A & P
my mother clerks in the baker-y
my sister dances in the hula show
and they do it for me, me, me

my old man's a psychiatrist
he has a psychiatrist's couch
he doesn't stick any needles in
but his patients still cry *ouch!*

he thinks I'm slightly paranoid
or maybe rather manic
I tell him I'll turn out all right
if only he won't panic

if you got anxiety
my dad will worry for you
at 25 bucks an hour
it's what psychiatrists do

★

Why?—Z
butter your bread
if you don't like it
go to bed

Why? Why? Why?
¿Cuándo? Pourquoi? Far vus?

why does a chicken cross the road?
no hablo español

waarom steekt een kip de weg over?
pourquoi non?

¿cuándo la gallina cruza la carretera?
vais ich?

perchè Garibaldi alla battaglia di Calatafimi
    portava le bretelle tricolori?
to hold his pants up, stupid

★

how and when and where and why
stars and sun and moon and sky

canals and craters, dunghills, dunes
tell me what's beyond the moons?

beyond the moons the sands are deep
they spread through all the purple skies
in them are Giants who never sleep
but watch the world with burning eyes

they're just like us, with sharper claws
huger pincers, fiercer jaws
and if they catch you—goodbye head!
goodbye little crystal bed!

so wrap your feelers round your feet
fold your thorax nice and neat
the sun is high, the hour is late
now it's time to estivate

    I lay me in my quartzy pool
    I pray the gods to keep it cool
    to keep off demons far and near
    and wake me when the winter's here
    to dance with joy on all my legs
    and live to lay a thousand eggs

*

    Mother Mother I am sick
    call for the doctor quick quick quick!!!
    Doctor Doctor shall I die?

    Yes my child and so shall I . . .

*Do you ever think when the hearse goes by
that one of these days you're going to die?
a-whoo, a-whoo . . .*

the dark the hairy scary dark's where
the nightblooming neuroses grow:

Mummy the THING'S under my bed again!

they wrap you up in a big white shirt
and cover you over with tons of dirt
a-whoo . . .

under my bed, my childhood bed
only the dustflocks blew
in the midnight caverns of my head
the goblins spawned and grew

they stuff you into a long long box
and cover you over with mountains of rocks
a-whoo . . .

but my children's fears are wider, wilder
fiercer, freer
in their delirious feverdreams
angry shadows chatter from the bookshelves
and Caesar's legions fight all Gaul from the staircase
landing
            imperial ibises rise
stark and threatening from the reeds of the rug

and the worms crawl out and the worms crawl in
and the ones that crawl in are lean and thin
and the ones that crawl out are fat and stout
a-whoo, a-whoo . . .

deposition by J.E.G., acquaintance of writer:

The storm was raging and the wind was howling outside the castle. Inside the castle the lights flickered of. There was a blood-curling shriek. A Black figure stalked up the corridor. Bloodstained was his hands. I ran down the corridor and fell. Quickly I got up. I ran down the corridor only to find a girl jabbed in the back. As I ran farther I fell in a pit. It was a donjon! I felt myself being chained to the wall. I struggled to free myself only to get whipped in the leg. The lights went on, I found the Black thing ready to cut my throat! I prepared to die. IM DEAD! IM DEAD! I screamed.

your eyes fall in and your hair falls out
and your brains come tumb-a-ling down your snout
a-whoo

Hap-py Birthday!
Hap-py Birthday!
children are crying
people are dying
Happy Birthday . . .

here you're in
there you're out
that's how the world goes
roundabout!

★

rise, Sally, rise
open your eyes
the earth turns east, the sun turns west
turn to the one you love the best

Red Rover, Red Rover, let Billy come over
I wish, I wish your wish may come true
the sun is up high at the top of the sky
you can't cross my river unless you wear blue

bushel of wheat, bushel of barley
all not hid, holler Charley!
bushel of wheat, bushel of rye
all not hid, holler I!
bushel of wheat, bushel of clover
all not hid can't hide over

look out, World! here I come!

we sing from near, we sing from far
you brought us here, and here we are

we sing from far, we sing from near
nobody told us why we're here

we sing by night, we sing by day
nobody told us what to say

in love begot, in lust begot
nobody asked us what we thought:

*

my warriors have pitched their tents
where Tigris meets Euphrates
I suck the stubborn teats of goats
and feed upon the date-trees

I hunker down upon my heels
(they call me chieftain's daughter)

and I crack my lice between my nails
and flick them in the water

    we have to sing, we sing a song
    it's all of Time and twice as long

*

    Black sheep, black sheep, have you any wool?

    Yes, Master Coxe, my fleece is fat and full

    Shearer, shearer, clip him to the fell
    and take the wool to little John who lives
      by the well

I sit and pick at wool
I pick at wool all day
I have no time to go to school
I have no time to play

the shepherds tend the flocks
the shearers clip their backs
and sell the wool to Thomas Coxe
who stuffs it into sacks

and when the bags are full
they bring them in to me
for every day I pick the wool
he pays my penny fee

my hands are cracked and sore
I pray to go to heaven
and hope perhaps he'll pay me more
next year when I am seven

I sing my song the whole day long
from morning light to even

*

I am a little chimney sweep
a poor benighted chap
I knock about the dark all day
and no-one cares a rap

the soot grinds down into my groins
each time my brush goes whap!
I'll die from cancer of the nuts
if I don't get the clap

    we sing our song, our song is long
    it's large as life and twice as strong

if you should see a chimney sweep
your luck will turn to bad
so always keep your eyes away
from a chimney-sweeping lad

but if by chance they light on one
don't let it go at that
—just hold your collar till you see
a horse, a dog, a cat . . .

*

    here upon the altar
    lies the bleeding victim
    we slew him without falter
    —that was why we picked him

    O mighty Rongo, here's your *fish*
    wrapped up in tidy parcels

was ever god served up a dish
of such prodigious morsels?

all the gods are bad ones
and some are worse than others
the god who gave me his name
had demons for his brothers

he chose the altar for me
the axe to split my head
the leaves to wrap my ears and nose
for the prize when I was dead

the missionary came then
and he took me in his arm
he swore *his* God would strike them dead
if they did me any harm

my father broke his spear in two
the prayer-king stove his drum
and as a joyful Christian child
I sing of Kingdom Come!

*

one day he gave me peaches
one day he gave me pears
one day he gave me fifty cents
to kiss him on the stairs

the missionary ladies
have taught me to sew and cook
to plant flowers in pots
and embroider French knots
and write in a bluelined book

they have taught me to read the Bible
and to frown and turn my back
on Corporal McGlash
when he twirls his moustache
and calls me the Rose of Ladakh

but my mother will come and fetch me
to my home on the mountain side
and I'll turn back my face
to the ways of my race
in Shamlegh when I am a bride

and turquoise and silver will bind up my hair
instead of a flowery hat
my three husbands will plough
while the fourth milks the cow
—but I won't tell the pastor that.

    I gave him back his peaches
    I gave him back his pears
    I only kept the fifty cents
    and kicked him down the stairs

*

Mammy, Mammy, tell me true
when shall we be free?

Hush, chile, eat you chickenfoot stew
don't say dem things to me
    ole Uncle Jack he wanta git free
    foun his way north by de bark on de tree
    cross dat river floatin in a tub
    paterollers gibm a mighty close rub

Mammy, Mammy, all de years
Massa laid us low

Hush, chile, hush chile, all you tears
won' make him let us go
   old Aunt Dinah jes like me
   wuk so hard she wanta git free
   but Aunt Dinah gittin kinda ole
   she feared of Canada cause it so cole

Mammy, wanta board dat Freedom Train
feel de sun shine on my haid

hush, chile! don' talk out so plain
or you mighty close to dead!
   ole Uncle Billy, mighty fine man
   tote de news to Massa, fast as he can
   tell Uncle Billy you want free fer a fac
   nex day de hide skun offn you back

and still we dance and still we sing
Juba dancers in a ring!

Juba dis an Juba dat
Juba skin dat Yaller Cat

Juba jump and Juba sing
Juba cut dat Pigeon's Wing!

Gadder roun, chillun, thank de Lawd
old Abe done set us free
Massa in de cole cole groun, praise Gawd
in de Year of Jubilee!

Missus an Massa, walkin down street
hans in dere pockets, nothin to eat
Missus git home, wash up de dishes!
patch up y'ole man's raggedy britches!

Massa run home, git out de hoe
clear de weeds outa y'own corn row
de Kingdom Come, de slaves gone free
ain no slaves in de Year Jubilee!

two four six eight
we don't want to integrate

   ('I dunno what they complainin about what with
   Bull Connor givin em free street
   baths an dog shows ever day')

put down you heel
put down you toe
   ever time you turn aroun
   you stomp Jim Crow!

git off you knees
hold up you head
   ever time you turn aroun
   Jim Crow dead!

★

get a piece of pork and
stick it on a fork and
shove it in the mouth of a Jewboy, Jew . . .

a skinny kid, a Yidl kid, I run the streets of Kiev
the sh'gutzim kick my shins, the cold winds blow me like a leaf
a skinny kid, a Yidl kid, with swinging black earlocks
for furtrimmed ladies and their gents my father fixes clocks
he cheats them just a little bit to make up for the tax
I call them *Pan* and *Panya* and I spit behind their backs
a dirty sheeny ragged Yid I spit behind their backs

Jewboy, Jew
Jewboy, Jew

I am Belsen number 7829
I know not blue sky nor to see the sun shine
blind, I hear others die. I am called swine.

and still we sing and still we sing
and through the wires our voices ring

does no-one hear? does no-one come?
Lord of the World, my mouth is dumb

*

Bach Jones a bag of bones
a belly full of fat
and when he dies he shuts his eyes
now what do you think of that?

in Aberfan where I began
I never grew to be a man
the slag ran down toward the town
I cried and I was still
God lost my name and no-one came
I died beneath the hill

still in their dreams our voices sing
through stone and slime the echoes ring

> Rhys Owen was a holy man
> he went to church on Sunday
> to pray to God to give him strength
> to whip the boys on Monday!

*

the light swings west, the shadows follow
the ball is hollow
on the wall

curtsey, salute and roundabout
we go by turns but never out

we turn the world away from night
we raise the sun, we bring the light

if we don't act the way we should
too bad for you. We're here for good.

and begin again